MW01241276

The 5 Secrets to Making Fast Changes for Good!

Dr. Dennis E. Bradford

Legalities

Conesus Lake, New York

Contents

Acknowledgements

I thank Christian Mickelsen for his inspiration and for the main outline of this book.

I also thank the many others who taught me how to master making major life changes including, but not limited to, all the authors of the books listed below in the Suggestions for Further Reading section; my great teachers including Karl Worstell, Art Spring, Don Sturtevant, Panayot Butchvarov, and Gustav Bergmann; my former colleagues including Bill Edgar and Carlo Filice; friends including Anna Foster; and many of my former students including Laura Simpson, Amy Glauner, and Deirdre Thorpe.

Of course, I alone am responsible for any and all intellectual, grammatical or typographical errors.

1

Intro to Making Rapid Change for Good

You are, or you should be, skeptical that making lasting improvements in your life or achieving major goals can be made fast. Typically, it's either impossible to achieve important lasting results, extremely difficult, or it requires years of effort. It always seems to be a frustrating journey.

You have likely failed. You have likely failed more than once. Are you pleased with your body fat percentage? Are you working at your ideal job? Do you enjoy great friendships? Are you in a great love affair? Have you started a business that is thriving? Have you achieved financial independence? Are you a great example for others, including perhaps your children? You've also likely observed many others who failed, too.

If so, we are alike. I, too, have failed and have observed many others who failed.

I kept thinking that there was something I was missing, some secret that would unleash a much higher quality of life that would last if only I could find it.

There's an enormous self-help literature. Judging from the number of books written on how to change life for the better in a lasting way, it's an extremely popular topic.

There is some objective statistical evidence available about some changes. It contains some good news. For example, in 1965 the number of U.S. adults who smoked was 41.9%. That dropped to 13.7% in 2018.

On the other hand, it also contains a lot of bad news. For example, 19 out of 20 people who significantly reduce their body fat fail to maintain that reduction for 5 years.

If there is a secret, it would seem that few understand it.

It's important to remind ourselves, though, that statistics don't apply to individuals. They only apply to groups. For example, if you are a smoker, either you quit or you don't.

The good news is that there is a secret. Most people don't appear to understand it, which explains why most people find making an important, lasting change to the quality of their lives either practically impossible or extremely difficult.

My chief purpose here is simply to point you in the right direction to uncovering that secret for yourself. While 4 of the 5 secrets may not be very secret, the 5th, which is by far the most important, seems little understood and it can yield instant improvement.

It doesn't matter what the change is that you desire. It doesn't matter what the goal is you'd like to achieve. It doesn't matter how many times you've failed in the past.

If you learn and begin using the 5 ideas presented here immediately, making important changes for good that last a lifetime can be not only satisfying but so simple that it sometimes seems almost effortless. You'll probably hit some difficult patches, but they don't last and following the 5 secrets will minimize them. The key is just to start to avoid the paralysis of endless analysis.

Once you understand the critical important 5th secret, you'll realize that it's been there all along. It's not new. What may be new is your understanding it clearly for the first time. In other words, all you need to do is to open to it. Opening to new ideas requires dropping attachment to old ideas. In that sense, **detachment is the key to successful, rapid, lasting change.**

It's nearly certain that you are locked in a conceptual prison and don't realize it. It reminds me of one of Winston Churchill's well-known statements: "Remember the story of the Spanish prisoner. For many years he was confined in a dungeon . . . One day it occurred to him to push the door of his cell. It was open; and it had never been locked."

Until we master the fifth and most important secret, we often fail because we try to do things the hard, wrong way. We try to do them backwards. Once we master the fifth secret, we begin to do things the much easier, right way.

The fifth secret is what is currently often talked about as an "inner game" secret. Although I find the inner/outer terminology misleading (because, as A Course in Miracles puts it "there is no distinction between within and without"), I'll here use it because it's at least somewhat popular and, so, perhaps not unfamiliar.

Physical changes are outer or external; mental changes are inner or internal. If we think of a human being as a skin bag of bones, blood, and flesh, what is inner is inside the skin bag and what is outer is outside the skin bag.

The hard way to change is from the outside in. The easy way to change is from the inside out. The hard way to change involves trying to force change from without. The easy way to change is to open to improvements from within. Therefore, we are a lot more successful at implementing any major improvement quickly when we work from the inside out rather than from the outside in. Of course, the improvement must be within our control; no amount of arm flapping will enable us to fly.

Outside changes are behavior changes such as forced environmental changes. They are sometimes able to produce lasting changes, but they are always difficult. For example, if you were imprisoned for the rest of your life and fed only 1200 calories of food daily, your percentage of body fat would not only drop but you'd maintain that lower percentage until death. Of course, nobody wants to do that even though it could involve achieving and maintaining a lower percentage of body fat. It's too hard.

A diet is a forced environmental change. That's why diets don't work in terms of stimulating a lower body fat percentage that lasts. Nobody goes on a diet for 5 years. The idea of going off a diet accompanies the idea of going on a diet. That's why informed nutritionists say, "Never diet." Any drop in your percentage of body fat due to dieting will only be temporary;

it'll go back up once you go off the diet. Instead, it's better to make small, permanent changes in how you eat that you can learn to enjoy for the rest of your life.

So, if your goal were, for example, to lose 50 pounds of excess body fat and keep it off for the rest of your life, should you go on a diet? Should you try to force change? No. Instead, learn how to eat well and over time drop foods that you shouldn't be eating from your nutritional plan and eat foods that you should be eating. That's much easier and much more effective.

I didn't pick that example randomly. It's likely that you've tried and failed to reduce your percentage of body fat in a lasting way. Again, 'lasting' here denotes a minimum of five years. If so, you have experience with how well forcing change works. It doesn't.

The real problem is one of "mindset." It comes from our rationality. It's perfectly rational to want to make the smallest changes possible that are necessary to produce the desired result. In other words, there's no reason to do more work than necessary. Laziness is rational.

[I discuss this in more detail in chapter 2.5 of Mastery in 7 Steps.] We assume that improving what we eat will result in lasting weight loss.

It's not that simple. It's not that difficult to go on a diet for 30 days or 90 days or even six or twelve months. You've probably done it and lost weight. That's improving what we eat, isn't it? How well does that work? It only works in fewer than 1 in 20 times for *lasting* weight loss. Furthermore, it's no fun and requires incessant vigilance. It's very difficult.

The reason why it's so difficult to lose a significant percentage of body fat and keep it off for over 5 years is because we tend to focus only on the outer game while ignoring the inner game.

Yes, the ideal purpose of eating food may be to attain as long and as healthful a life as possible, but, if we fail to master the inner game, we use food for a lot more than nutrition, don't we? For example, we sometimes enjoy binging on some favorite food or comfort eating. We also often socialize when eating and, so, distract ourselves from really paying attention to what we are doing with the result that we are not even conscious of how much food we are shoveling into our mouths. That's using food to provide satisfaction that has nothing to do with good nutrition.

The takeaway about eating well? If we neglect the inner game, our chances of ever achieving anything close to our ideal percentage of body fat and maintaining it for life are very small.

What's the much easier way? Work on the inner game first. The critical secret to making a lasting change as easily, effectively, and rapidly as possible is to focus initially on inner game mastery.

Living well is at least 80% inner game and the rest outer game. [I've explained this most recently in <u>Introduction to Living Well</u>.]

If so, the reason that most people never live well is because they either ignore the inner game or fail to master it. Please don't do that! If you master the inner game, you'll find that *everything* else in life becomes much, much easier.

Skeptical about that? That's fine. To be skeptical is just to be questioning and it's wise to question all my (or anyone else's) claims. I could write a whole book trying to convince you of its truth. However, many such books have already been written [see the Suggestions for Further Reading below that includes a number of them] and, after reading this book and implementing its ideas, you'll be in an excellent position to prove it to yourself.

Still, while being careful not to overestimate its importance, the outer game should not be ignored. The first four steps in what follows are outer game steps. Obviously, then, 80% of the five steps presented here don't involve the inner game.

80% of the value of here, though, comes from the last step, which is only 20% of the five steps. It's the critical one for success.

It doesn't matter – and I try to explain why in what follows – what we are trying to change: making lasting improvements depends on mastering the inner game. Whether we are trying to lose weight, find a lover, start a successful business, be a better parent, or anything else, whenever we ignore the inner game, our chances of lasting success are small (and, even if we achieve success, we'll have done it in an unnecessarily difficult way).

On the other hand, when we focus on inner game improvement, not only do our chances of making lasting improvements soar, but also doing that becomes as easy as possible.

It gets better: *if we improve our inner game, with the addition of just a little outer game work, that improvement will always serve us well in other areas.* For example, if you get your inner game right and permanently drop fifty pounds of excess body fat, might you be more likely to attract a good mate, become more noticed positively while at work, or be a better role model for your children? Of course! Others will no longer look at you and think anything like, "There's someone who is frustrated."

Yes, focusing on your inner game is uncommon in western culture. However, in just my lifetime it's become much more common. There is so much dissatisfaction and frustration experienced daily by ordinary folk that they know that something needs to be done; they crave change.

Outer game changes are not going to work for society any more than they work for individuals. (Societal outer game changes would be, for example, changing laws or governmental policies.) If enough of us as individuals will focus on improving our inner games, then, and only then, will beneficial, lasting societal changes occur. If we don't do it this century, I'm skeptical that human beings ever will.

Let me help you change for good in the easiest way possible. If you aren't interested in doing it for yourself, do it for someone else or for the rest of us. If you aren't interested even in that, please pass this book along to someone who might find it helpful.

Part I:

"Outer" Game

2

Get Clear about Your Destination

It's no secret that we are less likely to hit a target if we aren't even aiming at a target. Ask yourself: "What am I trying to do?" Whatever the answer, it will be something that you think would be good for you.

There are lots of things that are good for us. Pick one you find important as an example. With respect to it, about 2400 years ago, the great Greek philosopher Aristotle asked: "would not an awareness of it have great weight in one's life, so that, like archers who have a target, we would be more apt to hit on what is needed?" [1094a23, Joe Sachs, tr.]

The first of the five secrets isn't merely having a goal. The secret lies in having a crystal-clear goal. A common mistake is in not having a goal that is perfectly clear.

Let's postpone discussion of your most important goal until Chapter 7. Let's here pick a secondary goal as an illustration that's not only common but easier to understand without getting distracted.

Let's suppose you finally admit to yourself that you are too fat and adopt as your goal that of significantly reducing your percentage of body fat in a lasting way. Perhaps you've hit middle age and your metabolism has slowed so that you realize that you need to adjust your eating and exercising habits. Perhaps your physician has encouraged you to drop some excess pounds.

That's a laudatory physical goal. However, it's too vague. There are likely as many people in circulation as there are people who want to "lose weight."

Another common mistake is in thinking of a goal as fixed or static rather than as a direction. After all, life is a process that is in incessant flux. Another common mistake is focusing on a by-product of a result rather than a direction or process. In this case, there's no point going on a temporary eating and exercise program to attain a more healthful percentage of body fat if you later go off the program and regain probably wind up with an even higher percentage of body fat than when you started the program (even if your body weight is the same).

None of us can do anything sensible right now that will result in any significant fat loss. We only live now (in other words, we don't live in either the past or the future) and our power is always limited.

It's quite likely that you've heard of the S.M.A.R.T. goal setting process. It's popular with respect to reducing ineffective vagueness with respect to goal setting.

'S' stands for 'specific.' Be specific in setting your goal. "I want to reduce my percentage of body fat to 18% and keep it there" is more specific than "I want to lose body fat and keep it off." A specific goal is better than a vague one.

'M' stands for 'measurable.' In terms of what we do, it's easier to improve doings that are measurable than those that aren't. If we have a pair of plastic calipers for measuring body fat percentage, it's easier to keep track of it day after day than to reduce it without a way of measuring it.

'A' stands for 'attainable.' It's true that we often seriously underestimate what we're able to do, but setting unrealistic goals is a more common error. If you have never earned over $100,000 a year in your life and your goal is to make $10,000,000 a year by the end of next year, you may make it, but it's not realistic. A sufficient reason for that is that you simply don't control all the relevant variables about the economy.

'R' stands for 'realistic.' To continue with that example, a realistic goal for you might be to increase your yearly income to $150,000 in the next twelve months. You have already demonstrated that you have what it takes to earn $100,000 a year. Take the ways you've already been effective, learn additional ways from others or create such ways yourself, and work harder this year. Even if you fail and "only" increase your income by, say, $25,000, if you just repeat that performance in the following twelve months, you'll have hit your goal.

'T' stands for 'timed.' Without a time limit, we can all too easily procrastinate. If my goal in the weight room is a 1200-pound total (for example, hitting a heavy single deadlift of 500 pounds, a heavy single squat of 400 pounds, and a heavy single bench press of 300 pounds) and I delay until I'm 70 years old to begin training, I'll likely fail. So give yourself a realistic time period that stretches you but doesn't stretch you too much to attain your goal.

A problem we have with goals is that the S.M.A.R.T. protocol may not be applicable to them. This is particularly true with respect to important goals such as loving relationships. How does one measure love?

This is why it's really important to focus on the direction rather than just on the end result. With respect to lasting fat loss, it's actually achieved as a by-product of determining and executing an effective nutrition and exercise program that works well. It's just not possible to measure the direction as easily as its by-product.

Nevertheless, you'll improve your results, your direction, or both if you become as clear as possible about what you are trying to do.

3

Plan Your New Behavior – and then Forget the Plan!

I t's no secret that we are more likely to land at our destination if we have a plan for getting there than if we lack such a plan.

If I'm in Albany and want to drive to a conference in Chicago, should I just start driving and hope to find myself in Chicago before the start of the conference or should I plan my route? Obviously, I should plan my route. I'd drive to Syracuse, Rochester, Buffalo, Erie, Cleveland, Toledo, and South Bend to get to Chicago. It's easy with a map to measure the distance and estimate the driving time using, say, 50 or 55 miles per hour as an average. Without any mishaps, it'll take me about 14 hours of driving to get there.

To create a good plan, always start with the destination in mind. Allow a reasonable amount of time to execute the plan. It's wise to allow a little extra time to deal with any of life's vicissitudes that might arise along the way.

Especially if it's not something that you really relish doing, finding an accountability partner can be very helpful.

Then begin immediately to work your plan.

Now, please step back from this discussion and ask yourself: "How many times have I planned something like that and for some reason or other never reached my destination?"

If you are like me, the answer is, "Lots of times."

Because of that, you may now feel stuck, unable to go back into the past and change the results or to go into the future to guarantee better results. All we ever may control is the present moment.

This is why the second secret isn't in having a good plan. Planning is easy. How? Decide what you want. Decide when you want to have it. Work back from there to the present moment by specifying a clear, step-by-step process of actions that will get you what you want when you want it. Start immediately to execute that process – and persist until success.

The secret is to set a good plan and then to forget it! Why? That seems to make no sense.

Actually, it's the only possible way to be successful. When we're thinking of either the past or the future, we're failing to focus on the present moment. Since life always occurs only in the present moment, we're actually obstructing ourselves from doing what we should be doing.

Since we already have a good plan, we already understand what we should be doing. So, just do it. Anything, including useless thoughts about the past or the future, that obstructs focusing on what we are doing in the present moment should be dropped. Let go of all distractions and pay attention now.

That's counterintuitive, but it's the right way to execute a plan.

Why? Wouldn't it be better to focus on the plan? No -- as your own results probably attest.

You may know that some 25oo years ago The Buddha argued that the way to live well is to drop egocentric desires and attachments. If you want to live better, I suggest that you take that plan seriously.

Except for the desire for spiritual awakening (enlightenment, waking up) all desires are egocentric. [I return to this in Chapter 7.] They are for things that we want, crave, yearn for, long for, hunger or thirst for, have an appetite for, and so on. Given that, is it possible to desire what we already have or are? No. We're able to desire to continue to have it or to be it, but it makes no sense to want something that we already have or are.

Desires range from barely wanting something to obsessive craving. As psychiatrist David R. Hawkins, M.D., Ph.D., puts it in <u>Letting Go</u>: desire "is also expressed as greed, obsession, hunger, envy, jealousy, clinging, hoarding, ruthlessness, fixation, frenzy, exaggeration, over-ambition, selfishness, lust, possessiveness, control, glamorization, insatiability, and acquisitiveness." **To have a desire is to be dissatisfied**.

It's impossible to have a desire without being dissatisfied.

Desires obstruct freedom. To desire something is to be driven to attain it, to feel enslaved, whereas to experience freedom is to be able to choose or to reject without compulsion of any kind.

What's the problem with focusing on a plan to attain something? It's the usually hidden *assumption that the way to get something is to desire it.*

That's simply false. In fact, the stronger the desire to attain something, the more attaining it is blocked by that desire!

When we desire something, we don't do so freely. We are driven to choose it. We want it. We fear not attaining it. *Living in fear isn't living freely.*

When we live freely, we are free to choose what we want. When we live with a desire, it's false that we are free to choose what we want.

Goods come into our lives freely when we open to them. Goods manifest themselves in our lives effortlessly. If so, to desire a good is implicitly to deny that what we want is simply ours for the asking.

We've here touched on the most important theme in this book. **The way to live well begins with surrendering to reality just as it is.**

If this is a new idea for you, you should be skeptical about it. However, it's easy to prove to yourself. In this case, the way to prove it is simply to let go of your desires and notice how your life improves. The more you detach from your desires, the better you'll live. Instead of living in fear of not getting whatever you want, when you drop the fear you'll begin living freely and the goods you enjoy will increase as if by magic. The takeaway: Surrender completely to reality, to what-is.

Why does this work? Reality already is what it is. We often don't like it, but that's irrelevant. It is what it is. Resisting reality never works well. It can't. Since what-is already is as it is, resisting reality is futile and counterproductive.

If you don't like some situation exactly the way it is, if possible, try either to improve it or leave it. If that's impossible, accept it, surrender fully to it. The only alternative to that procedure is madness.

There's nothing wrong about having a plan to achieve something and then putting it into action while forgetting about the plan as you execute it. *What's wrong is assuming that some future situation will be better than the present moment.* True, you may prefer it, but it won't essentially be better. The present moment is the only moment we ever have to live and that assumption implicitly denigrates its value. No future moment is better than this moment. Or try thinking this way: since there are no future moments, this moment is the only moment we ever have to live.

If this strikes you as a strange idea, the reason is that you have become stuck on a radically incomplete understanding of what you are. What has happened is that you've become stuck identifying yourself with your thoughts, beliefs, emotions, perceptions, and experiences. It's true that they are part of you, but there's so much more than just that to what you are. **You are infinitely valuable**. Until we free ourselves from identification with the limitations of the egoic mind, we never realize that. Instead, we just keep living with the continual unease that comes from constant underlying fear. Instead of accepting reality, we resist it. That's the problem. [I point out in Chapter 7 how to solve it by, in effect, expanding what you take yourself to be.]

Improve Your Relevant Skills

Have you had difficulty making lasting changes or achieving goals? If so,
it's not uncommon for the reason to
be that you have not yet mastered the relevant
skills. Although this may not exactly be a secret,
it's often ignored.

Suppose, for example, that you are a single man
looking for a lover. Supposing you are straight,
where might you meet women? If it's in person,
how should you dress? If it's online, how should
you set up your profile? Do you understand what
qualities women initially look for in men? Have

you ever considered the fact that, since they are hit on daily in public, attractive women always have initial tests that candidates for their charms must pass quickly? What should your attitude be? How should you open a conversation? Should you use humor and, if so, what kind? Are you able to flirt well? Are you able to dance? Where should you go on a first date and where should you avoid going on a first date? And so on.

Suppose, for example, that you would like to have a business of your own. Would you be selling products or services? Should you have only a physical location, only an online location, or both? How should you market your business? What's the best way to use ads to attract prospective customers, patients, or clients without going broke? Could you get your business's message to the marketplace without increasing your ad budget (for example, by using publicity)? How should you receive payments? How should you set up fulfillment? How should you ask for reviews and solicit feedback? How should your business records be efficiently set up for accounting purposes? How could you grow your business? What should you look for when hiring help? And so on.

Whatever your goal, there are lots and lots of mistakes that it's possible to make with respect to achieving it. Therefore, although you may not have thought of it this way, developing your attitude about mistakes is also a relevant skill. Permit me three points about that.

First, *mistakes are inevitable*. Accept that. Why? It's because the future is unknown and unknowable. That's relevant because decisions that we make now always have future consequences and those consequences are, therefore, unknown and unknowable. [I return to this in Chapter 8.] That fact is part of our human condition.

Since mistakes are inevitable when it comes to making a lasting change for good, it's a mistake to think that they should be avoided. They cannot be avoided. That's impossible. Whether you do something or nothing, consequences will follow.

So, accept them as part of life. We all make mistakes. Fully accept that fact. Don't resist it.

Second, *keep mistakes as insignificant as possible*.

Isn't it obvious that the least costly way to do that is to learn from the mistakes of others instead of making all the mistakes yourself?

What's the fastest, least expensive way to do that? Read books by relevant experts. If you are going into a new field, begin by reading 5 or 10 quality books to begin to understand more about that field. You may be able to borrow them from a library without spending a penny. Even if you had to buy them new, spending $20 or $30 on a book can often easily enable you to avoid making mistakes that would otherwise cost you 10 or 100 or 1000 times that much.

I've had over thirty years' experience as a small-time real estate investor. In all that time, I only had 2 disagreements with tenants that landed in small claims court and I won both times. (Both happened in my first couple of years as a real estate investor when I was inexperienced.) In other words, I never had a single costly disagreement with a tenant. Furthermore, without exception I always made money buying or selling real estate. How? I began my career as a landlord by reading books about how to be a landlord. What sense does it make to become a real estate investor before understanding the basics of real estate investing?

Occasionally, I've had people tell me they tried being a landlord and had such a miserable initial experience that they soon quit. My simple question was always the same, namely, "How many books did you read about landlording before you began?" The answer was always a sheepish, "None." How foolish! A single mistake in real estate investing can cost tens of thousands of dollars.

Research. Learn. Think. Look before you leap. Don't be so foolish as to make all the mistakes yourself.

In addition to reading, and some people find it difficult to learn just by reading, there may be available courses and seminars that can really shorten your learning curve. They may cost more than reading, but, if you are able to afford them, they may shorten your learning curve so significantly that they may be worth it.

The fastest way to learn is to hire a one-on-one coach (guide, consultant). After an initial assessment, a good coach will be able to determine quickly which skills you need to upgrade to be successful and help you to upgrade them as quickly as possible. A good coach will help you minimize your mistakes and achieve your goal as fast as possible by personalizing an effective plan to make it as efficient for you as possible for you to do or be what you want..

If you have a job, you may have noticed that your business hires business coaches. If so, why? It's because they gain more from what those coaches teach than it costs them. It's often the same with good personal coaches. If you are seriously focused on achieving your goal as quickly as possible and you are able to afford one, I suggest seriously considering it. There's no better way to keep your mistakes small and shorten your learning curve.

Third, *don't repeat mistakes.*

Here's an interesting fact about life: when we make a mistake, life will keep giving us the opportunity to keep making it until we understand the lesson it's trying to teach us and stop making it.

So, whenever you make a mistake, and you will make them, ask yourself two questions: "What did I do well? What could I have done better?"

If you tried, you did well simply by trying. You probably also did other things well, too. The point of the analysis is not to beat yourself up; it's to improve what you are doing. Reminding yourself of what you did well and patting yourself on the back for doing it is a good first step.

The important second step is to try to figure out if there was something that you could have done better. If there isn't, forget all about the episode. If there is, absorb the lesson so that you don't repeat it and then forget all about the episode.

Christian Mickelsen likes to say that "the bricks of failure pave the road to success." Successful people in any field will confirm that.

If you are too afraid to make a mistake, you'll do nothing and, so, guarantee that you won't make any lasting change for good.

Welcome mistakes! They are concrete demonstrations that you are growing. Just keep them small and don't repeat them.

Of course, make as few as possible. As any successful athlete will confirm, the best way to do that is to hire a coach. If necessary, rely on books and courses to help you. When help is available, it's senseless to try to learn everything yourself.

Since we are protagonists in our own favorite stories, it can be very difficult to get accurate self assessments of where we stand, of our own virtues and vices. A good coach or friend can help us evaluate ourselves so that it becomes easier to strengthen our strengths and shore up our weaknesses.

It's a mistake to focus on eliminating weaknesses. Instead, just try to make them less harmful, which can sometimes be done by hiring someone else to do tasks that are not well suited to your aptitudes, and focus instead on improving your strengths. We all have strengths and they can always be improved.

It's often said that success leaves clues. Pay attention to them to make your path to lasting change for good as enjoyable as possible.

5

Create Your Optimific Environment

We are very susceptible to environmental influences. We are more susceptible to them than often we'd like to admit. When trying to make lasting changes for good, it's important to make it as easy on ourselves as possible to do that. Again, this may not actually be a secret, but it's often neglected. An idea is useless unless used. It's wise not to neglect optimizing our environments.

In fact, we should individualize them to make them optimific. There are usually physical, financial, or psychological limitations on our power to influence our environments, but that's not a reason not to try.

What is optimific is at least slightly different for each of us. Permit me some suggestions on some factors to be considered when trying to create an environment that makes flourishing as easy as possible.

Many, perhaps most, people have what Philip J. Goscienski, M.D., calls "a termite lifestyle." They don't notice damage until something collapses. We all have a choice not to live a termite lifestyle. How?

Become proactive physically. St. Augustine advises: "Care for your body as though you were going to live forever." In recent decades, scientists have learned a lot about eating well, exercising well, and sleeping well. There's no good reason now to struggle to try to learn for yourself those physical habits that promote good physical health, wellness, and pleasure. Avoid those that undermine physical well-being and adopt those that promote it. [My suggestions are in the 6th section of <u>Introduction to Living Well</u>.] If you're serious about living well, tend your body as if it were the only place you have to live. Why? It is.

For example, let's suppose that you are committed to reducing your percentage of body fat in a lasting way. Let's also suppose that you have a sweet tooth. Realizing that all carbohydrates, when digested, become sugar, should you ensure that you always have, say, plenty of delicious, high-carbohydrate snacks and desserts readily available? Of course not. Make it difficult for you to obtain them by keeping them out of your home so that you'd have to go outside your home to obtain them. Use laziness to your advantage and have on hand only, say, healthful snacks pistachios, macadamia nuts, or walnuts.

When, as will happen, your body becomes ill or injured, focus on helping it to heal. I suggest considering energy healing as well as traditional allopathic medical (pharmacological) or surgical approaches. [That fits perfectly with the inner game work discussed in Chapter 7 below.]

Become proactive mentally. Which predominant learning styles is yours? Once you understand it, use it to your advantage. Regularly feed yourself good mental nutrition. Deliberately set aside at least half an hour daily for learning.

What you consume mentally is at least as important as what you consumer physically. Since attention is the coin of the realm, be very selective about what you pay attention to. Focus on reading excellent books, taking excellent courses, and learning *only* from masters. Why? Life is too short to do anything else. So, let go of everything that is of less-than-excellent quality. Reduce entertainment to a minimum and carefully select your (few!) sources of news. Since it's always loaded with negativity and, so, depressing, going on a news fast is never a bad idea. Minimize consumption of anything that's less than excellent and uplifting.

The states of our lives reflect the quality of our minds. Ask yourself frequently: "How awake, conscious, free, loving, happy, peaceful, and creative am I? How could I improve?" As adults, we are fully responsible for our states of mind.

The most important lesson about living well that I've ever learned is that **living well requires mastering some spiritual practice or other**. (Don't confuse 'spiritual' with 'religious.') If you are sensing an imbalance in your life and have not yet mastered a spiritual practice, my most important suggestion to you is to find one that works well for you and master it. It's likely that you'd benefit greatly from either having help selecting one initially or having someone who is qualified help you to master the one you've selected.

Adding such a practice to your daily routine or increasing the effectiveness of your current practice is the single most important way to improve the quality of your life. Set up your environment to make it as easy as possible on yourself to practice. For example, suppose that your practice is sitting meditation. That need not take up much room. Have a small space in your home where your meditation mat and cushion or bench are always set up as opposed to having to set something up each time you want to practice. Make it as easy as possible on yourself to practice.

With whom do you choose to surround yourself? The people you associate with on a daily basis may be the most important part of your environment. Do you surround yourself with sages or fools? If fools, there's usually no need for dramatic changes. Just drift away from them gradually over time and drift toward sages or at least toward productive solitude.

If you have a choice (and most of us non-inmates do), it's wise to select very, very carefully the people who surround you. If you choose to surround yourself with either nonphilosophers or as-yet-unsuccessful philosophers, there's no reason to wonder why you have so far failed to live well. [See Chapter 7 below.]

A Specific Example.

J ay was 27 years old and afraid that he was going to have to live the rest of his life alone. He wanted a good wife and family. He was an eligible bachelor who couldn't seem to make a lasting connection with women. He was a certified public accountant with a good job at an accounting firm. He was personable and decent looking. He drove a 2-year old car and lived in a very nice apartment. He'd saved about $25,000 towards the down payment on a first house. Although he didn't really like them, he dutifully went out to clubs once a week. He'd had some hook-ups, but nothing lasted.

He was frustrated enough to have a strong desire to get this area of his life handled for good. He finally admitted to himself that there really might be something wrong either with him or with what he was doing or failing to do.

He went to a local bookstore and was amazed to find a lot of books on how to attract women and how to improve relationships. He bought one or two on how-to pick-up women and read them. Inspired, he looked online and found lots of courses and coaches offering similar advice.

Being impatient, he decided to go all in by hiring a personal coach. He knew that his accounting firm repeatedly hired business coaches and that they wouldn't do that if the rewards they received didn't significantly out-weigh the price they paid. He hoped hiring a dating coach would work for him. It did! He researched and found a suitable coach with whom he had good rapport. He hired him for $5000 for a 6-month one-on-one coaching program. Even before the end of the 6 months he had not only found a great gal, but they hit it off so wonderfully that they fell in love! He proposed to Pam and she accepted. Within five years they found themselves not only married, but also new homeowners with a 3-year old son. That reward was worth massively more than the cost of the coach.

Success, right?

Notice the outer game process that Jay followed. [i] He knew exactly what he wanted. [ii] Lacking a good plan to get it, he hired an expert to help him. [iii] His coach not only helped Jay improve some dating skills that needed improving but [iv] also had Jay improve his dating environment by exposing Jay to some better places than clubs to socialize and then helped Jay become comfortable there.

Yes, Jay enjoyed success. He gained the good wife and family he desired.

However, recall the old saying about being careful what you wish for. Is success all it's supposed to be? Often it's not.

The truth is that, especially when it comes to predicting how we'll feel emotionally, we are usually not all that good at estimating what future situations will be like.

It's not that Jay wasn't successful. He was. If you're an adult, you've undoubtedly known many people who were successful in many different ways.

The problem is that Jay's success was not built on a solid foundation. Jay assumed that getting a good wife and family would enable him to live happily ever after, but he was wrong. He had yet to understand a critical insight: **outer game success is always insufficient for lasting happiness**.

To begin to understand this more clearly, let's take a closer look at how Jay and Pam found themselves living five years after meeting. Determine for yourself whether or not it rings true to what you yourself have observed, or even experienced, about similar situations.

A typical day in Jay's life does not begin with him bouncing out of bed with a smile on his face. He's worries a lot about finances and tends not to sleep well. As an accountant, he knows that he's living on the edge of financial disaster. As if the monthly mortgage and escrow payment on their new house and the usual bills for insurance, food, automobiles, entertainment, and clothes were not enough, he worries about how he could ever possibly afford to pay for his son's college education. He and Pam want a second child as well. He hates the time he has to waste commuting back and forth to the office every day; it's unproductive and exhausting. He's come to resent having to wear business attire, too. There are always demanding and sometimes irate clients who need soothing. Tax season is the worst time of year, but, even outside it, his boss is hard on Jay. As a result, he works really hard and comes home mentally and physically tired. He suspects that Pam doesn't fully appreciate what he has to do at work to keep food on the table for the family, that she insufficiently appreciates his sacrifices.

Pam works hard, too. She's never enjoyed housework, but she makes sure that their home is always spotless and that their lawn and gardens are well tended. Her mother wasn't a great cook, so Pam has largely had to teach herself.

She shops for the best ingredients they can afford and always ensures that Jay has a good dinner every day. Of course, cleaning, planning, shopping, and cooking with a son in the terrible 3's is stressful. Pam knows that and tries to squeeze in some yoga when their son is napping. What really has begun to irk her is that Jay doesn't seem fully to realize what she does on a daily basis. It's seldom that she gets to lunch with friends like she used to do regularly. She's not able to get out of the house to take a course or go to a gym. She never seems to have sufficient time even to do the reading that she enjoys. She works tirelessly to make a good home and he almost never seems to acknowledge her efforts. Instead, he takes them, and her, for granted.

In short, they are both frustrated and resentful. Each harbors a secret grudge against the other. Each has anger about the way life has turned out. It expresses itself as coolness and correctness towards each other as they escape – he by watching television in the evenings and she by reading pulp romance fiction. Their sex life has deteriorated. Even though they share the same bed, they each retire to it alone. Each nurses unverbalized grievances towards the other.

That rings true, doesn't it? It's as banal as it is typical. Their marriage is headed towards a crisis that you can easily imagine for yourself.

Both Jay and Pam want to be acknowledged for their contributions. They each feel pressured. They each resist the pressure.

The typical result is emotional blackmail: "if you don't give me X, I'll punish you by doing Y." Y might be withdrawal, pouting, anger, having an affair, or filing for divorce. Nearly half of all marriages end in divorce.

Why? It's obviously not that people are unsuccessful at getting married. It's also not that people don't want to enjoy successful marriages.

The problem is that outer game success doesn't yield lasting happiness and most people focus only on the outer game. What Jay and Pam neglect is the same as what most of us initially neglect, namely, the inner game. They don't enjoy lasting peace of mind for the simple reason that they have never mastered themselves. (My suggestion? Jay and Pam should hire a relation-ship coach or marriage counselor to help them get on a better path.)

Is it possible to live well with someone else without first learning how to live well alone? No. Sorry, it's not. That's the important roman-tic delusion.

Notice that Jay started off from a position of need. He feared having to live alone with him-self for the rest of his life. He wanted to gain a wifeand family to fill the void in his life. He thought that would enable him to enjoy lasting happiness. In other words, his motivation was selfish, egocentric, self-centered. He wanted to use someone else to make himself happier.

Pam, too, let's imagine, wanted to use what is external to her, namely, another person, to create a loving family that she assumed would fix everything that was missing from her life, to fix herself. That never works for long and often doesn't work at all.

Falling in love has nothing to do with love. 'Falling in love' should be renamed 'falling in lust.' Traditionally, being lustful is a vice; it's not a virtue. Desiring someone is not loving that other.

Being successful is valuable, but it's of secondary, even peripheral, importance. The truth is that it's possible to live well without political freedom, good health, sex, money, power, fame, social status, and all similar goods. Success is insufficient for lasting happiness.

Furthermore, success is always precarious. **Whatever can be gained can also be lost**. If, say, you were to gain a lot of money or a great lover or a wonderful child or a mansion or political power or any similar good that you now lack and desire, wouldn't you always worry in the back of your mind that you could lose it at any time? In fact, don't you worry about losing goods that you already have?

Don't most people concentrate so much on being successful that they miss what is essential for living well? It seems so to me. In fact, in terms of living well or wisely, Jay's quest was doomed from its beginning because it was backwards: instead of looking to gain love, he'd have been better looking to love.

What's required for lasting happiness? Inner game mastery. That's why at least 80% of the value of this book relates to the inner game rather than to the outer game.

So, what's inner game mastery and how is it attained?

Part II

"Inner" Game

7

Get Right with Your Self

"Every art and every inquiry, and likewise every action and choice, seems to aim at some good, and hence it has been beautifully said that the good is that at which all things aim." That's the opening sentence of Aristotle's <u>Nicomachean Ethics</u> [J. Sacks, tr.], which is the most famous book of ethics in the western tradition.

It's the beginning of its second chapter I'd like you to consider carefully: "If, then, there is some end of the things we do that we want on account of itself, and the rest on account of this one, and we do not choose everything on account of something else (for in that way the choices would go beyond all bounds, so that desire would be empty and pointless), it is clear that this would be the good, and in fact the highest good."

Many goods we desire and act to achieve are not themselves intrinsically good. For example, you may work to earn money. It's good to have money, but why? Well, to buy food and pay the rent. What's good about having food or a place to live? Well, they promote health. What's good about health? Well, it promotes continued living. Such sequences stop at what is intrinsically good (valuable, preferable).

It's not just continued living that's intrinsically good. Otherwise, there'd be no suicides or even the thought of suicide. What's good about continued living? What is the highest good? Without being clear about that, we're living blind. We're making decisions about what to do or be without any ultimate target. It's insufficient just to answer that the highest good is a good life. That's true but it's terminally vague.

The inner game is really all about realizing the highest good. What's that?

In terms of answering that question, permit me to make a claim that you may find shocking: **We already are everything that we need to be to live well.** Our essence (nature, whatness) is divine. We are God in disguise. The critical problem is that we don't realize that.

Living well is not merely about thinking or believing that idea. Since a thought is just a conceptualization (judgment, proposition) and a belief is just a conceptualization that we attach to, thinking and believing are mental processes. By way of contrast, living well begins with "realizing" our divine nature. Realization requires getting out of our thoughts. Though not easy, the good news is that doing that is simple.

Mastering the inner game requires getting out of our thoughts into our lives. Classically, the way to do that for nearly everyone is by mastering some bodily (spiritual, energy) practice or other.

There's more good news: It need not take any time at all! This is the critical justification for using 'fast' in this book's title. None of the important ideas presented here are original with me and this one is no exception. For example, "it takes no time at all to be what you are" [from A Course in

Miracles]. If this makes no sense to you, it may be because you're falsely assuming that inner game mastery is an important gain and, so, will take time to accomplish. It's not. We already are what we need to be and realizing that is instantaneous.

Similarly, as the sage and psychiatrist David Hawkins similarly confirms: " . . . habits and behavior . . . can often be dropped, altered, or changed without undue discomfort . . . there may indeed be sudden changes in lifestyle, including major shifts . . . [from Letting Go]. Why? The key is releasing attachments. Ask: "How long does it take to drop something?" No time at all.

Even if all that's true and even though their domains are radically different, succeeding at the outer game and mastering the inner game often have similarities. For example, merely thinking is insufficient. For example, typically sustained practice of the right kind is required.

I'm not qualified as a spiritual teacher. Fortunately, since the time of the pre-Axial Age sages in India until recent teachers like Ramana Maharshi and Thomas Keating and contemporary teachers like Eckhart Tolle and the 14th Dalai Lama, there are a host of sages who have pointed the way. **Like success, mastery leaves clues**. If, as I hope, you want to understand more and look for relevant books, you'll have no difficulty finding them and I've tried to make it as easy as possible for you by listing some of the best in the Suggestions for Further Reading section below.

Want a sage to help you personally? That's much more difficult. They are available, but they are few and far between and can be very difficult to connect with one-on-one. However, there are certainly coaches available for hire who are able to get you started and point you in the right direction.

The famous philosopher Alfred North Whitehead wrote in <u>Process and Reality</u> that "The safest general characterization of the European philosophical tradition is that it consists of a series of footnotes to Plato."

He was repeated the widely held view that Plato was the first great philosopher in the western tradition. Plato was not only the first philosopher to ask all the right fundamental questions, but also he proposed brilliant answers to them. Of course, Plato had predecessors on whose shoulders he stood and many later philosophers (including his student Aristotle) have seriously questioned those answers. Still, there cannot be another first great philosopher in the western tradition. He was not only a master fundamental thinker, but he was open to Being and realized its importance for living well.

What does it mean to claim that Plato was "open to Being"? We are human beings. It's a fortuitous accident that in English we use the phrase 'human being,' which is easily interpreted dualistically, to describe ourselves. As animals, our lives unfold in the temporal domain of Becoming, which is characterized by the ceaseless flux of forms (objects, things). However common it is for humans to be stuck in Becoming, we are also able to access the formless, nontemporal (eternal, timeless) domain of Being, which is devoid of all forms and, so, all flux. I've argued in other books [for example, Introduction to Living Well and Are Your Living Without Purpose?] that living well, being wise, requires opening to Being. Not all seekers after wisdom do that, but Plato did.

From A Course in Miracles: "Being . . . is a state in which the mind is in communication with everything that is real."

The Buddha stands to eastern philosophy as Plato stand to western philosophy. In fact, my judgment is that he is the greatest philosopher who ever lived. Of course, The Buddha was a master thinker, a master of the philosophic dialectic, but more than any other great philosopher he successfully emphasized the critical importance of opening to Being for living well.

If so, there's no better inner game introduction than an initial exposure to some of the Buddha's valuable ideas.

According to his teaching, the way to live well is to commit wholeheartedly to seeking it, accept the truth about reality, and live accordingly. For example, "Take refuge in the Buddha, the dharma, and the sangha, and you will grasp the Four Noble Truths: suffering, the cause of suffering, the end of suffering, and the Noble Eightfold Path that takes you beyond suffering. That is your best refuge, your only refuge. When you reach it, all sorrow falls away." [From The Dhammapada, Easwaran, tr. Other direct quotations here are from this same work.]

There are different ways to interpret this. What does it mean to take refuge in the Three

Treasures? What do the Four Noble Truths mean? What is the Noble Eightfold Path? How could life without sorrow be possible?

Let's begin with an introductory answer to the last question. What was the Buddha's central project? What did he try to do? Etymologically, to be a philosopher is to be a lover of wisdom. Like all philosophers, he tried to figure out what living well or wisely was so that he and others could live well. He was not only wisdom seeker, he became a successful seeker, a sage. A sage is no longer a seeker. A sage is a successful philosopher, in other words, someone who is wise, who lives well, who is noble or superior.

None of us are born with an instruction manual for becoming wise. Realizing that we ourselves are not yet wise, how is it possible for us to determine who is wise so that we can learn from them? Yes, there are recognized spiritual teachers in our time as there were in the Buddha's time, but the only real way to find out whether or not their teachings work is to test them for ourselves.

At age 29 the (future) Buddha committed to philosophy, became a seeker and left his home and family. He wanted to live without sorrow, dissatisfaction, discontent. He sought wisdom. He was, as we know from how his quest turned out, a great spiritual genius. It only took him 6 years to realize nirvana, which is life without sorrow. At 35 he became a sage; he woke up. He spent the next 45 years until he died demonstrating to others how to live well and teaching them how to do it also.

To interpret the Three Treasures literally would be to claim that 'the Buddha' denotes the historical Buddha who lived some 2500 years ago, 'the Dharma' denotes his teachings, and 'the Sangha' denotes those people who practiced his teachings. It's more useful, however, for us to interpret them nonliterally. I suggest that we think of 'the Buddha' as denoting our Buddha-nature, the perfect enlightenment that is our birthright (whether we realize it or not), our essence or whatness; 'the Dharma' as denoting the undefiled purity that excludes nothing; and 'the Sangha' as the fusion of the Buddha-Treasure and the Dharma-Treasure.

The Buddha encourages us to free *ourselves* from the sorrow of worldly bondage. That makes sense, doesn't it? How could anyone free another? Since we cannot live another's life, if we are to live well, we must do it ourselves. "Now is the time to wake up . . . Sitting alone, sleeping alone, going about alone, vanquish the ego by yourself alone. Abiding joy will be yours . . ."

Permit me several points about this. There is no other time to live well than right now. There cannot be – ever. Since the past no longer exists and the future does not yet exist, it's always now. Therefore, either living well occurs now or it never occurs.

To vanquish the ego is to detach from ego-centricity. The ego may be understood in different ways. Here's how <u>A Course in Miracles</u> puts it: "The ego is the part of the mind that believes your existence is defined by separation." The ego is resistance to the unlimited, to Being. (Being is sometimes referred to as 'The Kingdom of Heaven' or 'God' or 'Love.') Vanquishing the ego is opening to Being. Being is characterized by limitless nonseparation. It's the source of all creativity as well as abiding joy and peacefulness. By way of contrast, the egoic mind is limited to Becoming. It thrives on separation, which is the cause of sorrow. Remember Being is without forms and, so, without separation. (That's why it's often also referred to as Emptiness or Void.) So, opening to Being undermines sorrow. Since living well or wisely is living without sorrow, opening to Being is the transition from being limited in Becoming to the unlimited bliss (abiding joy, infinite serenity, peace that surpasses understanding) of Being. It's breaking out of conceptual prison.

Therefore, the key to understanding The Buddha's ideas is the notion of waking up. Until we attain the perspective of a sage, we are "unconscious." Since consciousness is awareness, it might strike you as absurd if someone were to tell you that you are unconscious. After all, since you are perfectly conscious or aware of the claim that you are unconscious, that claim must be false. Well, no. It's just an analogy he's using.

Distinguish different levels. There's being in a dreamless sleep, which is being unconscious in the usual sense of 'unconscious.' Then there's being asleep and dreaming, which is a kind of confused consciousness. Then there's waking up from a dream into the everyday world in which we enjoy everyday consciousness or awareness. The Buddha's claims there's yet another level in which we "wake up" from everyday consciousness, superconsciousness.

Suppose, just for the sake of the argument, that there is such a state, that superconsciousness is real. If you and I have never directly experienced it ourselves, how could we tell if the Buddha's description of it as being without sorrow is correct? Obviously, we couldn't. Without experiencing it for ourselves, the best that the Buddha could do would be to try to point to it – and we might as easily misunderstand his analogies as we easily misunderstand his words.

It's not an accident that Plato told a similar story in Book VII of <u>The</u> <u>Republic</u>. Imagine that we were born in a cave and naturally took our experiences inside the cave to be experiences of the whole of reality. Now imagine that some adventurer, some philosopher, ventured outside the cave into a sunlit day and then returned to tell us about it. Could we understand him? Even if we could, would we believe him? Probably not, at least until we experienced the sunlight for ourselves.

Life in the cave is life in Becoming. Life in the sunlight is life in Being. Notice that there is dim light in the cave (candlelight in <u>The</u> <u>Republic</u>) and bright light outside, which may suggest that the two domains are in reality two ways of looking at the same thing. Note also that the task of the phi-losopher is not only to uncover and follow the way to live in Being but also to help others do so. Suc-cessful seekers don't just live for themselves by en-joying the sunshine outside the cave. They identi-fy with the as-yet-unsuccessful seekers remaining in the cave and deliberately return to them to help them help themselves also escape into Being. To love is to act selflessly in such a way as to benefit the beloved. Eternal Being is the source of (genu-ine) love. Love is union, oneness, the overcoming of separation. Again, there is no separation in Be-ing, which, to state it another way, is the source of the claim that God is love.

It may help to think of wisdom or living well as being in alignment with reality. Without direct apprehension of Being, there is no apprehension of ultimate reality. Without direct apprehension of Being, what we take to be real is actually much less than what is real. That's a valuable point to remember when judging others or less evolved versions of ourselves. They may be deluded, and we may have been deluded, but that doesn't make them evil -- only limited and confused.

The Buddha and Plato are pointing the way towards direct apprehension of Being and encouraging us to experience it for ourselves. It's critical that we take their teachings to be potentially verifiable. If we are seriously to benefit from them, we must ourselves become philosophers and open our hearts and minds. That may have been what Kant meant when he talked about waking up from his dogmatic slumber. To wake up is to break out of conceptual prison, to burst the limitations of discursive thought, to transition from thought to awareness. If we remain attached to our comfortable, habitual ways of thinking speaking, and acting, all we'll succeed in doing is to remain stuck in sorrow. Without practicing as instructed, without at least living the life of a serious seeker, we'll just remain stuck because we refuse to cultivate the way of living that is the sole purpose of their teachings.

Let's return to the Buddha's analogy that waking up to wisdom is like waking up from a dream. Notice that waking up from a dream requires more than just thoughts. Yes, we are conscious when we are dreaming, but how do we dream ourselves awake? How do we wake ourselves up from a dream? It's impossible just to think ourselves awake.

This explains why, contrary to the popular view, philosophy is not just about thinking well. Yes, it can be taught in a classroom. It's an academic discipline. However, it's much more than that. Its purpose is living well, not just thinking well about living well. The Buddha wasn't just a great thinker. He was a great human being, a sage.

In fact, he never wrote any books and one reason for that may have been that he didn't want people attaching to his thoughts. (Although Plato did write books, it was a similar tale because he wrote dialogues rather than monologues because he wanted to encourage others to participate in them to burst their own conceptual limitation.) Instead, he always instructed his students to find out for themselves. He encouraged them to get beyond thoughts into their lives by practicing well. Meditation was the chief practice he recommended. This brings us to the idea of taking refuge.

To interpret the idea of taking refuge correctly, instead of thinking of a refuge as a safe haven, think of it as a commitment. Taking refuge involves a continuing sequence of decisions to throw oneself unreservedly into practice-enlightenment. In Invoking Reality, Loori uses the analogy of a child taking refuge in a parent's arms — but think of the child as being at a dangerous height needing to jump to be caught by the parent. The child must trust unequivocally to jump, and, once the child jumps, there's no taking the leap back. (Similarly, Kierkegaard promoted the value of a continuing leap of faith.) Like the child, we, too, fear the consequences of taking refuge, of plunging wholeheartedly into practice-enlightenment, of letting go of all our many attachments, so we hesitate—at least until our realization of how much we are suffering and causing others around us to suffer provides a sufficient goad.

The so-called First Noble Truth is that living is difficult, imperfect, flawed. Usually, our lives are persistently and pervasively unsatisfactory. Sometimes our suffering is acute; sometimes we are on fire. Often, though, the misery is routine. Even moments of happiness are transitory and have a bittersweet quality; knowing they will soon end, we desperately cling to them. It's not as if our lives flow smoothly from one joyful experience to the next. Humiliation awaits each of us. Who among us is exempt from decay and illness? Who among us won't suffer the infirmities of age? Who among us won't die? Who among us has established loving encounters that are permanent? We are humiliated by being unable to control our destinies.

The Second Noble Truth is that it is our egoistic attachments, our narcissistic cravings, that make living difficult. As we continually ask of life what it cannot give, as we incessantly try to control what isn't in our power to control, as we are buffeted by one obsessive thirst after another, we hurt. It's our selfish desires that are causing us to suffer. It is our incessant delusive quest for permanent pleasures that is causing us to suffer. This is why living is difficult. The limited egoic mindset is what causes us to suffer.

The Third Noble Truth is that we have the option to liberate ourselves from life's difficulties. Freedom from our egoistic attachments, our narcissistic cravings, is possible. We can eliminate all the sorrow and suffering by eliminating what is causing the suffering. If we dissolve our egoism and our selfish desires, if we detach from our familiar attachments, we will find that we lack nothing. The more we deliberately counteract our normal psychological conditioning, the more peace we'll enjoy. There is a way to end our difficulties that will create lasting well-being.

The Fourth Noble Truth is that the way to realize this liberation is the eightfold Path. By cultivating a compassionate life of virtue, wisdom, and meditation, we can realize our inherent enlightenment. Living this path is living well. (Notice that this is not an accomplishment, something we gain or achieve; rather, it is a letting go of all the egoistic attachments that are blocking us from realizing our inherent nature.) What's the eightfold path? Its eight elements are Right View, Right Thinking, Right

Speech, Right Action, Right Livelihood, Right Diligence, Right Mindfulness, and Right Concentration. Each of them is in inter-being with the other seven; they are mutually reinforcing and complementary.

In the famous opening lines of <u>The Dhammapada</u>, the Buddha signals what is essential about the Eightfold Path: "Our life is shaped by our mind; we become what we think." Therefore, if we train (discipline, purify) our minds, we'll automatically be shaping our lives. This is why the wise shape their minds "[a]s irrigators lead water where they want, as archers make their arrows straight, as carpenters carve wood." If we don't train our minds, we won't live well; "no amount of penance can help a person whose mind is not purified."

How should we train our minds? By meditation. There is no other way: "There can be no meditation for those who are not wise, and no wisdom for those who do not meditate." Meditation is the paradigmatic spiritual practice. It purifies the mind by dissolving compulsive selfish attachments such as the greed, lust, hatred, fear, and selfish desires that generate most of our thoughts. The more letting go of our thoughts permeates our behavior, the better we live. "Meditation brings wisdom; lack of meditation leaves ignorance . . . there is no impurity greater than ignorance. . . Any indiscipline brings evil in its wake." An indiscipline is an attachment to a thought.

There are many kinds of meditation. They are all bodily or spiritual practices or trainings, such as aliveness awareness, zazen, t'ai chi, and qigong. It's important to understand that master meditators are always meditating. It's simple to become a master meditator, but it's never easy. Is it really surprising that it's difficult to wake up, to leave the cave, to train the mind? Though "a trained mind brings health and happiness," realize that "[h]ard it is to train the mind."

At this point in the dialectic an object may occur to you that presents an obstacle that can block the training process before it starts, namely, "Isn't it selfish to meditate? Instead of training (disciplining, purifying) my own thoughts, instead of trying to detach from them and let them go, wouldn't it be better to try to alleviate the sufferings of others?"

The Buddha's answer is negative. "Do not give your attention to what others do or fail to do; give it to what you do or fail to do . . . Before trying to guide others, be your own guide first." Why? A sage controls himself well, "meditates deeply, is at peace with himself, and lives in joy." Instead of merely telling others what to do, a sage shows others how to live well. A sage "is contented and lives a pure life of selfless service" that is "[f]ree from the desire to possess people and things"; he lives "[w]ith friendship toward all." This is the better way to help others.

Ultimately, the way to alleviate the sorrow of others is to identify with them. If we remain attached to our ego's, to the egoic mind, we're blocked from identifying with others and remain separated from them. Waking up from thoughts is letting go of egocentricity. When we do that, we open to love. To love another is to identify with that other, to treat that supposed other as oneself. What appear to be two are in reality one.

Sorrow is created by separation and ended by union. Love is union, the opposite of separation. What sages do is to identify with others, to take those who are supposedly separate as themselves. Therefore, sages are the greatest lovers.

Nonsages don't do that. They identify with what they take to be their own persons, which are their own thoughts, perceptions, emotions, beliefs, and so on. We all have a choice: we can remain stuck as persons or allow person-hood to dissolve into sagehood. Ultimately, if the Buddha is right, there's separation between persons. Since it's always separation that creates sorrow, there's no sorrow when we detach from separation. Since direct apprehension of Being dissolves separation, that is what is required to live peaceful, loving lives of abiding joy.

Therefore, inner game mastery is required for living well. Inner game mastery is realization of nonseparation. Without it, even if there's out-er game success, separation remains. If there's separation, there's sorrow. If there's sorrow, out-er game successes are hollow and without last-ing satisfaction.

8

Bonus

Assuming, as I hope, that your self-esteem is sufficiently high that you want to improve the quality of your life, what should you do next? It's impossible to know.

The thought that there is a right or wrong action is just another thought from which it's wise to detach.

It's not difficult in this case to understand why. Suppose you are thinking about whether or not to do something. Call it 'X'. Can you know if X would be right or wrong?

Whatever X is, it will have (future) consequences depending upon whether you do it or not. Are those consequences relevant in evaluating whether or not X is right or wrong? (They may or may not be the only consideration concerning the rightness or wrongness of X, but do they count at all?) Yes, of course they are relevant. How could it be possible to judge correctly the rightness or wrongness of any action without at least taking all its consequences into account?

Can you know those consequences?

Actually, when 'know' is used in the strict sense in which knowledge is the inconceivability of being mistaken, the answer is obviously 'no.' There's no certain evidence sufficient for knowledge available about the future for the commonsense reason that predictions about the future may also be mistaken.

Well, then, is there at least rational opinion about all those consequences? Again, no. Why? They are merely imagined consequences. Since the future doesn't exist, they don't exist either.

Furthermore, even if there were rational opinion about some of those consequences, could there be rational opinion about *all* of them? Way leads on to way. What about those consequences that will eventually occur in, say, 50 months or 50 years or 50 million years? The truth is that we have no idea what they might be.

So, although this idea may initially shock you, there's no way that we can have either knowledge or rational opinion about the rightness or wrongness of some contemplated act.

This idea shouldn't shock you. It's been around for a long time. For example, it's the reason why the oldest Zen document from ancient China reads in translation as: "If there's a trace of right and wrong, / True-mind is lost, confused, distraught" [Sengcan]. It's only nonsages who think in terms of right and wrong.

We have little choice but to act in our daily lives as if the future will be like the past even though there's no epistemic warrant for doing so. The greatest English-speaking philosopher was David Hume. He argued that our thoughts about the future are only justifiable psychologically.

Conjunctions of event-types are, at best, only constant conjunctions and there's no reason other than psychological habit to justify the belief that they'll continue to go together in the future.

For example, I expect the sun to rise tomorrow morning. Why?

Well, I've been noticing now for quite a few decades that it rises in every morning. Do I know that it will rise tomorrow? No, because I am easily able to think of how I could be mistaken. It could blow up tonight and, if it does, there'll be no rising sun as seen from earth tomorrow morning. In fact, there'll be no morning. Is it rational, though, to believe that it will rise tomorrow? Even if it were rational to believe something that might be false, the event in question is merely an imagined one. There is, as yet, no tomorrow. In that sense, is not my belief about a nonexistent event? Unless it were a necessary truth (such as *red is a color* or *a square has four sides* or *3 is less than 5*) how could it be rational to believe anything about a nonexistent event?

Idiotic politicians are constantly trying to tell us to adopt their favorite programs about what is right or wrong to do. For all I know, they actually believe what they say. Let's, though, admit the truth and not emulate their <u>hubris</u>. Let's not be as foolish as they are. Thinking we know what we are doing is a vice, whereas epistemological humility is a virtue.

It's impossible, then, to think our way to practical morality, to determining the difference between right and wrong acts. Since there's no knowledge or even rational opinion about right or wrong acts, let's detach from that idea and instead emulate sages. Right acts do not come from thinking about right acts. Instead, they come from no-thought, which is the state of consciousness that results from waking up from thought. No-thought awareness is super-consciousness, which is alert awareness without thought or tension. Right acts are selfless and spawned by no-thought.

Therefore, it really is impossible to think through what you should do and justify a decision about what to do or not to do.

Please remember that when you are judging the actions of others or even your own. As long as we restrict ourselves to the domain of thinking, nobody has any answers. In that sense, we are all in the dark, we are all limited. Again, this makes forgiveness a lot easier, doesn't it?

Is there a better alternative? Yes, there is: break the bounds of discursive thought. Obviously, we cannot think our way to doing that. We need to drop thought and act based on no-thought. When it comes to interpersonal encounters, that's acting out of love, out of identification with the other, in other words, acting without separation.

You could, if you wanted, emulate the Buddha or Plato. (That's been my way. Even since I discovered philosophy as a teenager, I've always had the feeling that, had it not existed and had I'd been bright enough, I'd have invented it!) When they admitted to themselves that they both wanted to live well and didn't know how to live well, they became philosophers. Unless living well happens by accident, seriously trying to live well by committing to a life of philosophy is the first step.

Obviously, succeeding, becoming a sage, is the second step. The idea is not to spend life endlessly seeking. If they are right, the third step is waking up from the dim light in the cave into the sunlight of Being. Living well, doing better, begins with that realization about Being. It's capable of indefinite expansion.

You may be wondering about me. I became a philosopher in 1964. I obtained a doctorate in philosophy in 1977. I've been meditating daily since 1994. That's been my way.

What's yours? What should it be?

Unless you have a better idea, I recommend the first step. Commit to living well even if you don't know what that means. It'd be wise for all nonphilosophers to become philosophers. Everyone should be a philosopher!

If so, where should you begin? Start from where you are. Since you already are reading this book, if its ideas resonate with you and are at least beginning to make some sense, you could start simply by reading the books in the "Suggestions for Further Reading" list below.

You could take relevant courses, too. How is it possible to tell in advance which courses are relevant and, even if you find some, which teachers or professors will prove effective for you? That's a problem.

Perhaps, you already know a sage to emulate or could locate one who might give you some personalized tips. However, if you are not yet yourself a sage, how could you recognize someone else as one? It's not always easy. Even if you found a genuine sage, there's no guarantee that he or she will be willing to guide you personally or that you two will ever establish an effective rapport and good working relationship.

For some students, especially those beyond the undergraduate years, a better way than either reading books or taking courses, if you are able to afford it, might be the fastest way, namely, hire a personal coach. A personal coach need not be a sage. The idea is just to find someone with whom you can establish good rapport who can help you select a direction that might be most fruitful for you and help you gain initial traction.

It's easy to find helpful outer game coaches. Christian Mickelsen claims that it's the second-fastest growing industry now in the U.S.

It's more difficult to find a helpful inner game coach. Why? It's much easier to become successful at one aspect of life than it is to master life by becoming a sage.

Here's a sufficient answer: it's well known that Hume wrote: "Reason is, and ought only to be the slave of the passions, and can never pretend to any other office than to serve and obey them." If so, emotions are more fundamental than thoughts. Consider, then, deliberately tending to them at least as much as you tend thoughts.

The degree of wakefulness or superconsciousness is what is of critical importance if you are looking for a sage or spiritual teacher. (The Buddha distinguishes 4 levels.) The more awake, the better. How, though, is it possible for nonsages to recognize those who are sages? It's not. Sadly, there is no standard certification and there are con artists in every field.

Again, though, the personal help of a sage is not necessary in the beginning. (All the sages I've personally known began their quests by reading books or taking courses.) An initial good guide, though, can be extremely helpful. How might you recognize one?

My suggestion? Contact some without spending any money and try to determine the degree of emotional rapport between the two of you. If someone is a con artist in a field in which you're not an expert, that person will more easily be able to con you on the level of thoughts than on the more fundamental level of emotions. So at least have a conversation with that person and "listen" to your gut.

If so, although it's certainly a good idea to straighten out your thinking by reading books and taking courses by those who have mastered the art of thinking, it may be an even better idea if you want fast results to find a guide with whom you are quickly able to establish a connection that feels right from an emotional point of view.

Permit me a final suggestion that won't cost you a penny and less than 44 minutes of your time. If you follow through and do what I recommend, you'll begin to undermine two important obstructions to living better, namely, too much stress and too many prolonged un-wanted emotions. Stress depletes our energy and emotions such as shame, guilt, grief, anger, and fear weight us down. By diminishing or eliminating those two obstructions, you'll find it easier to improve the quality of your life.

Here's a webinar training that I did recent-ly that you may register for and watch at no cost:

https://event.webinarjam.com/register/2/452gmug

Furthermore, at the end of the webinar I of-fer you yet another bonus, namely, the possi-bility of having me teach you how to dissolve any prolonged unwanted emotions you already have – again without your spending a penny!

Those bonuses will, if you make use of them, reduce stress as well as emotional distress. There are, though, other obstacles that you may con-front. If they are acute, I encourage you to get some temporary help from elsewhere – a life coach, a consulting philosopher, a psychiatrist, a clinical psychologist, a spiritual teacher, or even just a wise friend. Also, begin immediately to read the books on the reading list below. Using the bonus teachings and executing these two suggestions may be sufficient to provide you with effective help to enable you to continue your evolution to living better.

I hope that you've found reading this book stimulating and helpful. If so, feel free to recommend it to others. I thank you for your attention and wish you all the best.

Dennis E. Bradford

Conesus Lake, New York
15 Aug 2022

Suggestions for Further Reading

Abram, D.	The Spell of the Sensuous
Anonymous	The Bhagavad Gita
Anonymous	The New English Bible
Anonymous	The Upanishads
Aristotle.	Nicomachean Ethics T. Irwin or J. Sachs translation
Borg, M., ed.	Jesus and Buddha: The Parallel Sayings
Bradford, D.	3 Common Myths about Emotions that Keep Us Stuck!
Bradford, D.	Are You Living Without Purpose?
Bradford, D.	Emotional Facelift

Bradford, D.	<u>Introduction to Living Well</u>
Bradford, D.	<u>Mastery in 7 Steps</u>
Bradford, D.	<u>The Meditative Approach to Philosophy</u>
Buddha, The	<u>Basic Teachings of the Buddha</u>. G. Wallis, ed.
Buddha, The	<u>In the Buddha's Words</u>. B. Bodhi, ed.
Buddha, The	<u>The Dhammapada</u>, E. Easwaran, tr.
Buddha, The	<u>The Dhammapada</u>, G. Wallis, ed.
Butchvarov, P.	<u>Being Qua Being</u>
Butchvarov, P.	<u>Skepticism in Ethics</u>
Butchvarov, P.	<u>Skepticism about the External World</u>
Butchvarov, P.	<u>The Concept of Knowledge</u>
Campbell, J.	<u>The Hero's Journey</u>
Chaung Tzu	<u>The Essential Chuang Tzu</u> Hamill and Seaton, trs.
Csikszentmihalyi, M.	<u>Flow</u>

Dogen	<u>Shobogenzo,</u> Nishijima & Cross, trs.
Elkrief, N.	<u>A Guide to The Present Moment</u>
Ferguson, A.	<u>Zen's Chinese Heritage</u>
Frankl, V.	<u>Man's Search for Meaning</u>
Graham, ed	<u>Disputers of the Tao</u>
Hanh, T.N.	<u>Being Peace</u>
Hanh, T. N.	<u>Old Path White Clouds</u>
Hanh, T. N.	Teachings <u>on Love</u>
Hanh, T. N.	<u>Zen Keys</u>
Herrigel, E.	<u>Zen in the Art of Archery</u>
Hume, D.	<u>A Treatise of Human Nature</u> P.H. Nidditch, ed.
Kabat-Zinn, J.	<u>Wherever You Go There You Are</u>
Kant, I.	<u>Critique of Pure Reason</u>
Kapleau, P.	<u>The Three Pillars of Zen</u>
Kasulis, T.P.	<u>Zen Action Zen Person</u>
Katie, B.	<u>Loving What Is</u>
Kornfield, J.	<u>A Path With Heart</u>

Lao Tzu   _Tao Te Ching_ J. Starr, tr.
Leonard, G.   _Mastery_
Loori, J. D.   _Invoking Reality_
Loori, J.D.   _Riding the Ox Home_
Loori, J. D., ed.   _Sitting with Koans_
Matthews, A.   _Follow Your Heart_
Martin, R.   _The Hungry Tigress_
Millman, D.   _Way of the Peaceful
                      Warrior_
Nagarjuna   _The Fundamental
                      Wisdom of the Middle
                      Way_, Garfield, ed.
Nietzsche, F.   _Twilight of the Idols_, R.
                      J. Hollingdale, tr.
Nisargadatta M.   _I Am That_
Norretranders, T.   _The User Illusion_
Plato   _The Collected
                      Dialogues of Plato_
                      Hamilton & Cairns, eds.
Plotinus   _The Enneads_ S.
                      McKenna, tr.
Rahula, W.   _What The Buddha
                      Taught_
Reps & Nyogen, eds.   _Zen Flesh, Zen Bones_

Rochester Zen Center	*Chants & Recitations*
Ruiz, M.	The Four Agreements
Sangharakshita	The Three Jewels
Sartre, J-P.	Being and Nothingness
Sartre, J-P.	The Psychology of Imagination
Sartre, J-P.	The Transcendence of the Ego
Schucman, H. [scribe]	A Course in Miracles
Seligman, M. E.	What You Can Change . . . And What You Can't
Smith, H.	The World's Religions
Sumedho, A.	The Way It Is
Suzuki, S.	Zen Mind, Beginner's Mind
Taylor, S.	Waking From Sleep
Thorp, G.	Sweeping Changes
Tolle, E.	A New Earth
Tolle, E.	Stillness Speaks
Tolle, E.	The Power of Now
Wu, J.	The Golden Age of Zen

There are also plenty of free talks by recent and contemporary sages on YouTube. Depending upon your learning style, you may find them even more helpful than reading books. I particularly recommend those by Eckhart Tolle, David R. Hawkins, and Thich Nhat Hanh.

Made in the USA
Middletown, DE
05 November 2022

14173501R00056